HOW TO QUIT SMOKING

EVEN IF YOU DON'T WANT TO

SOLUTION AHEAD

INCREASE SPEED

By Barbara Miller

Please share
Barbara Miller

1

Order this book online at www.trafford.com/00-0008
or email orders@trafford.com

Most Trafford titles are also available at major online book retailers.

Note for Librarians: A cataloguing record for this book is available from Library
and Archives Canada at www.collectionscanada.ca/amicus/index-e.html

Printed in Victoria, BC, Canada.

COVER DESIGN BY ROBERT FISHER

ISBN: 978-1-55212-344-7

*We at Trafford believe that it is the responsibility of us all, as both individuals
and corporations, to make choices that are environmentally and socially sound.
You, in turn, are supporting this responsible conduct each time you purchase a
Trafford book, or make use of our publishing services. To find out how you are
helping, please visit www.trafford.com/responsiblepublishing.html*

*Our mission is to efficiently provide the world's finest, most comprehensive
book publishing service, enabling every author to experience success.
To find out how to publish your book, your way, and have it available
worldwide, visit us online at www.trafford.com/10510*

www.trafford.com

North America & international
toll-free: 1 888 232 4444 (USA & Canada)
phone: 250 383 6864 ♦ fax: 250 383 6804
email: info@trafford.com

The United Kingdom & Europe
phone: +44 (0)1865 722 113 ♦ local rate: 0845 230 9601
facsimile: +44 (0)1865 722 868 ♦ email: info.uk@trafford.com

10 9 8 7 6 5 4

** Dedicated to **

Dr. Darryl Sinclair
my dentist who discovered my cancer,
which changed my life into one worth living,

and

BB. Your love served me well:)

ACKNOWLEDGMENTS

If I was born to be a mountain climber I would have said "I want to see what's at the top." I refer to my life's journey as a climb to the top of the "mountain of my choice". My main motivation came from wanting to live by example and to demonstrate what is possible. I had all the odds stacked against me but that didn't matter to me. I would not have been able to get this far without the following people in my life.

Many thanks go to the Minister at the Baptist Church in Prince George who in the late 60' taught me a child of five years old the power of forgiveness. Without that my journey would have never started.

In the early 70's I met Yvonne Kennedy who would turn out to be the best big sister from the YWCA a young girl could ask for. I didn't have a mom growing up but Yvonne and her husband Bill showed me a side of life I really needed to see. Yvonne I know you think this is too much but you are the foundation of my soul. Bill, you where such a good role model and you didn't even know it but you where. Without this role modeling I would not be who I am and this book would never have been written.

To a man named Akbar also in Prince George who said to me in the early 80's, "If you do anything in this world, read." I did just what you said Akbar, I did read. I started reading at age eighteen books that shaped me into the person I am today. I continue to read even now. It has been the best advice in my life so far.

My heart goes out to Norman Vincent Peal, Dale Carnage, Stephen Covey, Anthony Robins, Dr. Wayne Dyer, David J. Schwartz Ph.D. Patrick Fanning, and Matthew McKay. They are among the many people who have inspired me, shaped me and helped me in ways I am sure they can not fathom.

Mary Mohr my Page Maker, who has been described as a "true mom". What can I say? It's true. If I had an ability to have chosen a mom it would have been you. You are not just my page maker you are what a true spirit of giving looks like. This book project is forever in your debt. I smile whenever I think of you. Her son Clark Mohr was such a big contributor. It was his idea for me to ask Mary to be my Page Maker! Good idea Clark, I love your mom and I love the fact that you where unwavering whenever I needed any help.

From the Women's Business Network in the early 90's, is Barbara Coultish Past President whose efforts to assist me went a very long way in creating my DVD, The Choices You Make part of a live workshop that comes from this book. Also past President is Ester Hart who was my mentor and friend and one of three editors of this book project. There is a special place in my heart for these fine ladies.

Stella Scrimger was tireless in editing and a big support as well as her son Malcolm Scrimger, who was a monumental help in the early stags of my career. His friendship like his mothers' will never be forgotten.

To my best friend Debbie Hatten Waters, Debbie you saw me go though some really hard times and you where there at the front lines in a way that no one else could have been. When you need me I will be there!

Alan Klughammer is a great photographer www.klughammer.dnsalias.com and a good friend and someone who also knows the true spirit of giving. A special thank you for the photo shot on the back cover.

Also a good friend is Mickey Cherneski who has helped tremendously in the editing of the 2nd edition and also my Home Study Edition that comes from this book. This is just more proof that we don't get to the top without good people in our lives.

I met my mom when I was nineteen and we have had a great relationship since then. People often ask me if I am mad at her for not being there when I was younger. I am not. I never have been and never will be. I am my mother's daughter and I am just like her. I feel like I completely understand her choices. She may not have been there when I was a child but she has been there for me in a big way as an adult. My brother Al has been a big supporter to my goals as well. Even though they are listed almost last in my acknowledgments they are first in my life. Thank you Mom and Al, I know you love me as I do you. I love my oldest brother Andy too.

My father was a locksmith and I have dedicated page 33 to him. He lived by example and showed me the path to being my own boss.

Wim Borsboom, is a very gentle soul who sees auras. He told me to give myself credit for how far I have come in life. Now that I appreciate how far I have come I am able to go on to the future. *This time I am taking me with me!* Wim, you have touched my heart like no other.

I am not sure if you can imagine how hard mountain climbing is. I needed to be strong and courageous and I could not have made it this far without the combined support, love and encouragement of these wonderful people. You are all very special and dear to me.

Table of Contents

Part One ~ The Beginning Stages

Part Two ~ The Key to Change

Part Three ~ Your Mind is Like a Computer

Part Four ~ Don't re-invent the wheel

Introduction

They'll tell you that in order to quit smoking you have
to want to. Well, I disagree. You must, however, admit you are
willing to change. Quitting smoking is about changing, period.
This book is about how to do it. I didn't want to quit smoking,
I enjoyed it. What motivated me to change was I wanted to
live a healthier life-style.

In order to change you must have a plan. What are you
going to do first? This book is the master plan that will help
you to get started. It can also help in other areas of your life you
might like to change.

The first segment allows you to continue to smoke while
you examine several things such as looking at your reasons for
smoking and what could motivate you to change. Also, what do
you find is the most difficult part of quitting? That question and
more are dealt with. You will learn how to be a happy nonsmoker,
when the best time to quit is and the first part of getting ready for
the change. Getting ready is an important part of this program.
How can you do anything if you are not ready?

In the second segment I'll tell you one of my favorite
secrets, one I highly recommend, even though many quit smoking
programs do the opposite. I guess I'm a rebel. This secret can
help you deal with approximately 75% of your withdrawal
episodes. You'll have to trust me on this one. Try it and you'll
see that I'm right. Also in this segment you'll learn why many
smokers procrastinate and you'll learn about will power. You
don't have to worry if you don't have any because I'll show you
how to get it, grow it and fine-tune it.

You'll have to look at and examine your beliefs that make you who you are. It's amazing how beliefs impact our life. *I enjoy smoking* is a very destructive belief. I'll show you how changing beliefs can change your life. This is not complicated and can be fun and enlightening. You will uncover what really motivates you. I will also share one of my most powerful visualization strategies that did wonders for my motivation. It scared the heck out of me! At this point **you will anticipate quitting.**

This part of my program is where you will learn about the power of suggestion and self-hypnosis. For those skeptics out there, please give this a chance because it's different from what you might expect. This whole program is about learning and changing from within. When you're finished you will end up with a one of a kind product made for you and by you. Throughout this program you will have to do several exercises that will give you all the information you need to make your own recorded tape.

Yes that's right. You'll need to make a tape that will have all the information you need to successfully stop smoking. Your voice will be in the form of you talking in a hypnotic tone. The reason this tool is so effective is because you will be in a very relaxed state of mind. You will be talking to you, the *"you"* you want to become. I will show you how to make real what you want to be real and make true what you want to be true.

One of my best examples is on my tape. I told myself that the smell of smoke wouldn't bother me. Well, it's true. The smell does not bother me. I also put on my tape "I never really enjoyed smoking." The subconscious does not know the difference between the truth and a lie. In this segment I'll give you all the information on how to make a powerful, *self-designed, self-hypnotic* tape that you will listen to when you are ready to quit smoking. It will in fact be the most effective tool you'll need to get you through the tough times. When you're finished all the exercises in this book you'll have something concrete you can carry with you.

Because this is not a cold turkey program you will have a formula for your final days as a smoker. This powerful formula makes quitting more comfortable than you could ever imagine. So do not dread quitting. By the time you get to this part you'll see and feel how easy it can be. I hope along the way you enjoy my humour.

In part four you'll find my personal story, including some of my exercises. As well there is an inspirational story and some comments I hope will motivate you.

> **For those of you who say you don't want to quit smoking please turn to page 45. I understand how you feel about not wanting to quit. This section will shape you into the person who will choose to make empowering decisions.**
>
> **When you have finished all the exercises in this section start back at the beginning of this book.**

For those of you with even a small desire to quit, please read this book in the order it was written, as this is a step by step plan that starts now. Good luck, get ready and hang on. You're going on a ride that will change everything!

How to quit smoking using the BMP Method.

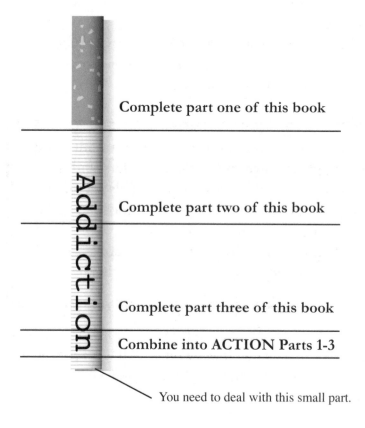

Complete part one of this book

Complete part two of this book

Complete part three of this book

Combine into ACTION Parts 1-3

You need to deal with this small part.

When you have completed all this work and decide to take action by implementing the BMP Method into your everyday life you will have the keys to breaking free.

Myth– Quitting smoking is as difficult as quitting Heroine.
Truth– Nicotine is as addictive as heroine. You can die coming off heroine.

An ambulance will not come and get you while dealing with nicotine withdrawal.

PART ONE

THE BEGINNING STAGES

What is the Difference?

It's no secret that there are many different approaches to quitting smoking. There are also many ways to lose weight. A common thread is that nothing will happen unless a person is willing to change. Give yourself some bonus points for having this book in your hands, as it is a good indication you are a willing participant.

I would like to point out something special about my program. But first let me ask you, do you know what the patch, hypnosis, gum, acupuncture and other gadgets all have in common? Well, they are products and services people go out and buy or obtain. They are external products you try to internalize. An example is the gum. You go to the store, buy it and put it in your mouth.

> **My program is developed to get you to go within yourself and bring valuable information out.**

When you are finished all the exercises in this book you will have a one-of-a-kind, tailored, homemade product. **Be prepared to work! It's better than a trip to the store!**

What makes my program special is I will show you how to make the necessary changes from within. The power to change doesn't come from the drugstore. The answers you are seeking come from within. This is why the exercises in this book are very important for you to do. You must get this vital information out of your head, onto paper, for your own eyes to look at. It will not be effective if you only mentally do the work. Even if you're a bit reluctant please go and get a pen and some paper and get ready to work. Doing this work is a small price to pay for making quitting easier.

> **PAPER WORK = QUITTING MADE EASY**

The Dreaded "Reformed Smoker"

I'd like to explain the term "reformed smoker". People say there's nothing worse. I believe the worst part of a reformed smoker is that they are walking around as living proof that it is possible to quit. I imagine for some, who believe in their addiction, this poses a threat. Another thing you may want to consider is, giving "reformed smokers" a bad rap could be used to create pressure for you not to quit and stay in the smokers group. It's that good guy, bad guy thing.

I'm sure you have had a bad experience with one or two, or you know someone downright self-righteous. This bad attitude gives all reformed smokers a bad rap. The truth is, we're not all bad. You don't have to be either. I would like you to know harassment is a form of peer pressure. Many people started smoking because of peer pressure. In some cases these same people were pressured into quitting. They think "if it worked for them, the same tactic might work for you." I admit I was pressured and it did help me want to change. Peer pressure is a powerful thing. Some choose to act in a rotten way. Either way, the reason they do it, tactful or not, is because they care about you. Even though it may not appear that way at some level, they do in fact care. Why else would they give you the time and energy?

Please remember, it is important for you to know a bad attitude doesn't come about simply because you quit smoking. Heck, some people just enjoy complaining.

Your goal is to become a nonsmoker. Wouldn't you like to get familiar with what kind of "reformed smoker" you'll become? I want you to know how to become a happy nonsmoker.

This is part of the plan in getting ready. First, before you do anything, you must decide that when you're ready to quit smoking you are not going to go around whining and complaining about others who still haven't quit. Your mind is like a computer. You're making a new program. This program is marked non-complainer! That's it! All you have to do is simply decide.

Make a vow right now that when you quit you will be a happy nonsmoker.

I bug smokers in a positive way.

All the exercises in this book have to be completed. If you are finding you having trouble with this work and/ or being self motivated perhaps you can show this book to your employer and they can decide to implement this method for all staff who smoke and I can assist you in a live workshop. If you do not have employment or a supportive employer you can contact me directly to arrange to be in a group or a one-on-one session. bmpmethod@shaw.ca

Choosing the Best Time to Quit

Is there a good time and a bad time to quit? If so, then when is the best time to quit? How do you know if you're ready? In this program I refer to quitting as the **LAST PACK.** It is the final part of the plan where I will show you how to use your last pack. In this segment I want you to know when is the right time to open it. I often refer to opening this pack or quitting as **"GO FOR IT!"**

There is a good time and a bad time to make this move or to "go for it". Conditions must be in your favor. Are you in a bad relationship? Could you imagine trying to quit then? Would you try to quit if you just lost your job? Do you think drinking alcohol could affect your chances of being successful? There must not be anything going on in your life that disrupts the natural flow of what is normal for you. Another example is getting a raise. This isn't normal as it doesn't happen every day. Normal is having a consistent period of time where there are no highs or lows. **If you have something in your life that is causing you bad stress then you must look at eliminating that stress. If it is your job that is causing the stress and you can't leave then you must learn how to handle the stress more effectively. Ultimately nonsmokers are more relaxed because they have a way of calming themselves from within, rather than looking for an alternative outside of themselves.**

This is life's ups and downs.

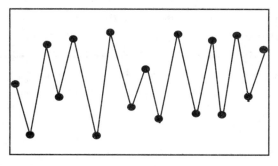

Quitting is not recommended at this time.

17

This is life - coasting along.

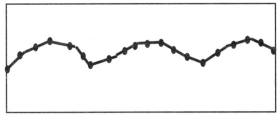

Master
the art of
relaxation.

By tuning in to your environment and being aware of your stress levels and eliminating them (or managing them) you are indeed getting ready for the last pack. You must do this before you "go for it". Eliminating all stress will ensure a better chance of success. **When you have mastered this, all is calm in your life and you are doing all of the work in this program consistently, you will start to develop a "feel" for when that time might be.** This feeling you'll get is like a window of opportunity. The feeling will build and build as you simultaneously manage your stress and stay on my program. This build up is a feeling like a strong propulsion. A jet has this and so does a high performance boat or a race car. What do they all have in common? They go a long way in a short amount of time. It's compacted energy. So is the mental propulsion that pushes you into a state of will power that is unstoppable!

This program is designed to help you get ready too. While you work on the outside conditions in your life you can simultaneously do the work in this manual and prepare for the internal (mental) aspects of getting ready.

I can't stress enough the importance of doing all the written exercises and following through with the plan.

> The plan is designed to cause some discomfort and even anger towards your smoking habit and is partly responsible for the mental propulsion that takes place.

Stay on the plan and you will feel when the time is right to "go for it". In the meantime work on making your life relaxing.

An exception to the rule

The rule is "calm and normal". Well there are exceptions to the rule. To quit successfully under stressful conditions is possible, however you must be very strong and emotionally hang on and fight with all you have. The most important thing you can do for yourself is just to be prepared. Have you ever been on a roller coaster ride? If you have you knew you would be scared but did it anyway.

I know it's possible to quit under extreme stress as the last time I quit I found myself in the middle of it. I was living with my boyfriend and three other roommates. It was a five- bedroom house and I was in charge of running things, on top of a full time job. I was on my "last pack" when things fell apart in my relationship. I needed to end it. The boyfriend insisted that he continue to live there as a roommate. What a joke! What was I thinking? He kept trying to get back together. There was no way it was ever going to happen. He brought women over to try to make me jealous. We would argue at length. The police came and horrendous name-calling went on inches from my face. It was ballistic and nothing short of a nightmare!

I quit smoking in the middle of it all. I did not want this man to interfere with such an important issue and I became even more determined. I could not let this guy get the better of me so I dug in and hung on. I made it! What a victory it was! If you're on your last pack and something happens don't give up! It is possible to just hang on and ride it out like a bad storm. Anyway it's good practice for the next bout of stress.

You are more likely to succeed however, in a calm environment. If stress shows up and you don't make it that time don't give up. Keep doing the steps in my program and don't beat yourself up over feeling like a failure. You're farther ahead for trying than if you didn't try at all.

You are more likely
to ride out a
wild storm of stress
if you are
prepared mentally.

This book will show you
how to do it.

This is not "Cold Turkey"

My definition of "cold turkey" is "cruel and unnecessary punishment" How long have you been smoking ? Has it been three, five, ten, twenty years, or more? I am not going to tell you it doesn't matter because I believe it does. How long you've been smoking determines the bond you have with it. Your mind, body and life-style have come to know tar and nicotine. You went through a process in forming the habit. Since then you have gotten unreasonable change for cigarette machines, stood in long lineups and probably borrowed money for cigarettes. Over the years you've traveled together, gone through life's ups and downs together and partied all night long with them. You have kept them through thick and thin! You can't just give them up, can you?

If after reading this plan you decide to go cold turkey I applaud you as I think it requires so much more mental stamina, making the toughest times almost unbearable. I have also heard that the chances of starting again down the road are very high. I've talked to people who have successfully quit cold turkey. I ask them if they still crave cigarettes and they say that, yes they do, all the time.

I believe cold turkey leaves the brain with an unfinished business feeling. It's like there is something unresolved going on. Perhaps it's like a sudden death. There is no closure, no chance to say good-bye. My program is designed so there is no after taste. When you're done you will be really done! How do we do it? …**Get ready to change!**

Smoking is a relationship with tar and nicotine.
In this program you are preparing to part ways.
How long you have been smoking may determine how
long you will be on this method. In fact what you are
doing is getting ready to say… GOOD-BYE

Prepare Your Mind

Please get a pen and some paper. If you don't you might as well give this book to someone who will not be so stubborn.

Exercise 1
- Write down how long you have been smoking .
- Next write how much you smoke in a day, a week and a month.
- Calculate your weekly cost and your monthly cost.
- Multiply your monthly cost by twelve.

Example

One pack a day = $8.00 x 7 days = $56.00 a week

$56. x 4 weeks = $224.00 a month

$224. x 12 months = $2,688. a year

To get an accurate yearly figure you could also multiply $8.00 by 365 days = $2,920. Add extra if you lend them.

If you are not smoking a pack a day divide the amount of smokes in a pack by what is cost to buy. Figure out what one cigarette cost to get what you spend per day/week/month/year. Example- .40 cents divide by 10 smokes = 4.00 per/day

Were you aware of how much money you are spending? Keep these amounts fresh in your memory as you go through this program, even if it doesn't seem like a lot of money to you.

I recommend you open a new bank account. Why would you be angry about quitting when in 5 years to will have how much money?

Why Is Quitting So Hard?

Exercise 2

If you were to quit smoking right this minute, what would cause you the most problems? Think about it and feel it. What would be the hardest part? Write as many answers as possible. What fears do you have?

- Are you afraid of the anxiety you felt the last time?
- Are you worried you will become a raging maniac?
- List the cigarettes that would be the hardest to give up.
- What obstacles can you foresee?
- Write down what really bothers you about quitting.

The purpose in doing this work is to jump into the future, find the problems, bring them to the surface, expose them and eliminate them!

Example

- My biggest problem is I don't feel I'm ready.
- I'm worried I'll fail.
- I'm scared I'll be awful to be around.
- What if I can't do it? I have so much dread.
- My morning smoke, after a shower
- After a meal smoke
- The smoke I have as soon as I get into my car
- Talking on the phone could be an obstacle as I smoke a lot then.

When you look at your problems objectively you can now begin to find solutions. Then when you are ready to "go for it" you will have eliminated all the major foreseeable problems. If you do all that, I'm sure you can see how much easier quitting will be.

Solutions

- I will quit when I feel confident.
- I vow not to be a crabby jerk to be around.
- I'm going to deal with my favorite smokes while doing this program. In the end they will not cause me any problems.
- When I'm ready to quit smoking I will avoid the phone as much as possible.
- I will skip the little rest I have after the shower.

What you are doing is getting prepared, while allowing yourself to still smoke. Do you smoke first thing in the morning? When you quit, would waking up be your first obstacle? If so, then what you need to do is eliminate this problem now, by not smoking for at least 20 minutes after you wake up. If this is a big challenge for you start with ten minutes. Your next goal is one half an hour then one hour then two hours. **The ultimate goal is four hours.**

Success breeds success.

When you realize you can go half an hour without a smoke you will begin to feel good about yourself. This feeling will bring confidence and you will then go on to your one hour goal. Each time you become successful at increasing your time your confidence will build. Try it. It feels really good. This same idea applies to your entire problem, or habitual cigarettes. Do this same thing with your after meal smoke. When you get in your car do not smoke for ten minutes. Come on! I know you can make yourself wait! It's not that hard. Get a watch if you need to. Think about it. If you can't go without for four hours, how on earth are you going to quit for good? Start practicing now!

This part of the plan takes effort and discipline on an on-going daily basis. Once you incorporate it into your routine it will become easier. Before you know it, you will not miss the morning cigarette. When that happens you are well on your way to getting ready to quit. Can you see how by eliminating the problems quitting can be more manageable? Can you feel the dread leaving? Confidence will replace the dread.

Congratulations for making yourself wait! Do not reward yourself and smoke two in a row! The other benefit in this is to cut down the amount you smoke in a day. Not only that, but you also get to smoke lighter brands.

Good for you if you are already smoking a light or ultra light brand. If you are not please do so.

I know you might not like this part of the plan but it is important for several reasons:

1. You're not expected to like it—causing frustration.
2. At first you might smoke more—costing more, causing more frustration.
3. Switching to a lighter brand sends confirmation to your brain of your intentions to quit.
4. It is a major shift in the norm—an interruption of habit.

Exercise 3a

In your mind's eye go into the future. You didn't do the work listed here in this book. You continued to smoke for another five years. Write down what your life is like. What will it be like in ten years if you have not quit? On paper imagine still smoking fifteen years from now. Go-ahead, close your eyes. See yourself still smoking. Now write a small paragraph about what you saw. How much will you have spent in 5, 10, 20 years? Use your numbers from pg.22 I promise it's better than a trip to the doctor's office.

This exercise will be recalled for future use. They are like pieces to a puzzle. At the end you will see the whole picture.

Exercise 3b

- Write a paragraph about why you absolutely must quit. (Someday).
- Use as a reference. (exercise 3a)
- If you have a problem with using your imagination think of **what would make you want to quit?** Repeat this question over and over. The answers will come to you.

Make a list of the many reasons you can think of why you want to become a nonsmoker. Put some effort into this list and challenge yourself to see just how many reasons there are. You can compare your list with my list of reasons located on page 90. The general rule is to keep this list in the positive. Spend fifteen minutes comparing exercises 3a and 3b.

You can double your reasons for quitting by looking at the positive and the negative. "I will not waste money" is just as good as "I will save money".

A Mental Challenge

I said you could keep smoking. I didn't say it was going to be enjoyable. If you have ever attempted to quit before then you know what a painful and frustrating experience it is. It's like a mental battle.

**The objective in my method
is to transfer this battle.**

You will experience it while you are smoking instead of when you are quitting. If you want quitting to be easier, then smoking must become harder to enjoy! Can you imagine how much easier quitting could be if you took all the enjoyment out of smoking? Lets say there is only a small part of you that would like to quit. If you took away the fun and only smoked because of the addiction part, a larger part of you would want to quit. You then realize having the addiction is not fun either. By knowing and feeling this, smoking will become easier to let go of.

Are you ready for the challenge? This is a very important step so please take it seriously. First, say out loud " I am going to quit smoking some-day!" Good, now say it again. Did you say it like you meant it? Fake it if you must, but sound like you mean it. Second, starting right away you must say "good-bye" to your current brand of cigarettes. You must alternate every time you make a purchase. This means if you are smoking a pack a day, then every day you will buy a different brand. This is a good time to switch to a light brand if you haven't already. Or you can go ultra light if you are already smoking light.

There are several reasons for this step. They are all equally important. They are listed below—

- *"Let go"* — causes discomfort. It is amazing how attached you can become to a brand name. It says something about who you are. People who smoke Export "A" are tough. The Marlboro man was a cowboy, and on and on it goes. When you "let go" of this "brand" you are well on your way to letting go of the addiction as well. Such a simple idea, yet it can cause some major discomfort. Keep in mind, this discomfort is there now so it will not be there when you quit. Take this opportunity and marvel at this discomfort. Keep doing this step and you will soon anticipate quitting instead of dreading it.
- *"Break-out"*—Creates awareness. It is so habitual to buy the same brand day after day. You need to interrupt this auto pilot thinking.
- *"Not fun"*—You will also become conscious of your smoking because it won't "taste" the same or "feel" the same. It's not the same. It's not intended to be.
- *"Bad taste"*—You will smoke it anyway. You paid for it. This may anger you as you smoke something you don't really enjoy. Direct this anger towards the addiction.
- *Confirmation*—Stepping out of the auto pilot mode sends a signal to the brain of the intent to quit. Every time you purchase a different brand you are reminding yourself you want to change. When you buy your smokes, remind yourself that you are doing it because you are going to quit some day. Repeat this thought over and over.
- *Discipline*—Putting in this continued effort requires discipline. This is great practice! At times you may find this step difficult. Force yourself to do it anyway. This exercise of discipline will come in handy when you open your "last pack".

When you combine all of these reasons and put them into practice you will begin to change. You will look at smoking in a whole new way. You will feel differently towards smoking. The addiction will stand apart from the enjoyment you used to have. Do not be surprised if doing this step causes you to feel angry. This is normal and to be expected.

Are you going to smoke for the rest of your life? No? Then that means you're going to quit some day. If you're going to quit some day then start with getting rid of your brand. If you can't do something as simple as that, how on earth are you going to quit? You are aware of how difficult that can be. Do this step and quitting will be anticipated not dreaded.

There is another benefit of letting go and disassociating with your brand. When you have finished your "last pack", are out with your friends and see your old brand, you'll not think twice about it. Your heart won't even skip a beat. You will not give it another thought. If you skipped this step and were able to quit, there is a good chance that seeing your brand will bother you. It is kind of like an old friend who wants to rekindle the relationship. You will need some extra will power every time you see your brand. Save yourself some grief and get rid of your brand now!

If someone enquires about your brand, tell them you are going to quit some day and that you are getting ready to make some changes. Do not tell them you are on a program. I will explain the reason for this later on. For now it is a good idea to tell every one about your intentions. If they ask when, tell them "when the time feels right".

What do you do if you roll your own? Stop rolling and start spending more money. Then you too can alternate brands. What, can't afford to? Think of it as an investment. Spending money on tailor-made cigarettes will cost more creating even more anger and frustrations. If you can't afford tailor-made cigarettes then think of the money you will save if you don't smoke at all.

What do you do if you already alternate brands? Is it ultra light? Are you alternating every time? If they're regular size then switch to king size. Then you have two choices. One, you can pick one brand you don't really like and stay with it. Or two, you can alternate between your three least favorite brands.

I knew a woman who rolled her own cigarettes and she also put rosemary in them. When I told her my plan she said, "Oh I couldn't smoke without my rosemary." I smiled and said, "Good, then quitting will be easy for you".

Review

1   Let go of the image your brand gives you.
2   Create an interruption—get off the autopilot.
3   You can smoke but it will not be enjoyable.
4   Constantly remind yourself of your promise to quit.
5   Create an opportunity to discipline yourself.
6   Realize the power of #1-5 all added together.
7   Don't try and find excuses why you can skip this step.

Exercise 4

Take some time to describe what being a non smoker will feel like. What will this be like? Take your reasons for quitting and make it read like a story. Feel the sense of accomplishment. The key to this exercise is the emotion. Make all your benefits of being a non smoker in the positive.

Example

Negative form - **I will not** be controlled by tar and nicotine.

Positive form - **I will** be in control of my life and be free of tar and nicotine.

Negative form - **I will not** be wasting so much money.

Positive form - **I will** save a great deal of money.

(Use your focus number pg 22)

> **THINK ABOUT WHAT YOU WILL BE GETTING**
> **AND NOT WHAT YOU ARE LEAVING.**

Remember this exercise and all the ones before it will be used later on in another part of the program. The work is being spread out so you will not have to do it all at once.

I am aware this is work. You may be reluctant to do it but it is important to remember *that this information is vital in the process of making quitting easier.* You may find this mental work hard and not enjoy it. This is the price you pay for getting yourself in this predicament. You got yourself into this situation. **You can get yourself out.** The way to do it is in this work I'm insisting you do.

The answers you need are inside of you ~
not in the drugstore!

> **Put down the book and do this exercise**
> **and the ones before if you haven't already.**
> **In the end you'll be glad you did.**

You need to be a self starter to be successful at the BMP Method. If you find that you are skipping ahead and not doing the work that you are being asked to do then consider showing this book to your employer and asking them about having BMP Productions come in and perform a one day workshop. Not working? See www.quitsmokingbmp.com and find out if and when BMP Production will be your area.

Part one summary

- Go into yourself not the drugstore.

- Vow to be a happy nonsmoker.

- You will "feel" the best time to quit.

- This is not "Cold Turkey".

- How much are you spending?

- Expose and eliminate problems associated with quitting.

- Get prepared to quit.

- Interrupt the norm.

- Cut down the number of cigarettes.

- Choose to smoke a lighter brand.

- Transfer the battle of quitting.

PART TWO

THE KEY TO CHANGE

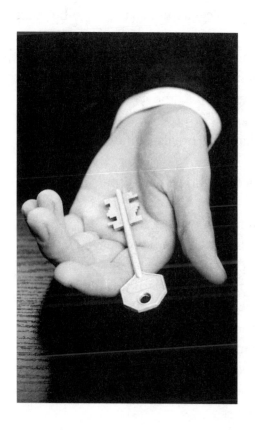

Privileged Information

You are going to have privileged information. This part of the plan is so much fun. But, unless you try it you'll never know.

The plan:
When you are ready to open your "last pack" you must not tell anyone! Do not tell people you are quitting or that you are on your "last pack".

This privileged information is to be guarded like a very private secret. I'm sure you have had secrets before and you just had to tell one person. It is O. K. to share this with one person if you absolutely must. If you do, you must be careful to pick the right person. In a little while I will tell you why this secret is so important. For now we must go over choosing the right person to share this privileged information with.

- Someone who will be supportive about your decision to quit
- Preferably a nonsmoker
- A person who can honor having privileged information
- You must not live with this person (no exceptions)
- Consider a person who lives out of town.
- You must not work with this person.
- Someone you do not see every day
- Pick someone you admire and respect

Have you ever told someone you were quitting smoking? Did they laugh at this idea, or were they supportive and encouraging? Have you ever heard, "Yeah, and I'm a monkey's uncle."? This one was popular in my day. It is amazing how many people do not encourage people who wish to quit.

Other quit smoking programs suggest you tell lots of people that you're trying to quit. I completely disagree! Yes, you will tell them you are going to quit some day. They do not need to know when you are going through this personal ordeal! When you tell someone about your personal plan to quit smoking and they do not praise and encourage you they can rob you of will power and confidence. It is not worth taking the risk because you need all of the confidence you can get. This is a very important part of my plan.

There are several other reasons why this is so very important. They are:

- ◆ Trade. Have a secret instead of a cigarette.
- ◆ When you are ready to quit smoking and you want to "go for it" you will then open your "last pack". If you tell someone you are quitting and they see you smoking, they'll comment and say, "I thought you were going to quit?" or "I knew you couldn't do it." You do not have the energy to waste on explaining yourself. When you are ready to "go for it" you will be focused on your plan. Hearing negative comments or wasting energy explaining things would distract you.
- ◆ Holding onto this secret will be fun. How long will it take before anyone notices? Could you ever imagine quitting smoking could be fun? Well, trust me on this. It is so much fun to see how long it takes people to notice! Also, because you are protecting your secret and acting "normal", the more people don't notice the more it makes you smile. It's like you have something up your sleeve. This is why I refer to it as privileged

information. You have it and they don't. The attitude
— "I know something you don't know" is a suave, sly
kind of attitude that makes going through the quitting
mode a whole lot more fun.

♦ You have finished your "last pack". You are a bone fide
non smoker. How are you going to act? Do you know
how to act as a non smoker? Act "normal". Act as if
everything is fine. You will have to if you want to protect
the secret.

♦ You will not be able to seek out sympathy. This is the
price you pay for getting involved with smoking. You do
not get to go around and tell everyone how hard it is to
quit. Doing that is what makes quitting so hard. When
people seek sympathy they are setting themselves up for
a fall.

You will have anticipation!
**With this plan in place you can look for-
ward to quitting, as you know this time
it will be easier.**

Eliminate 75% of the Nicotine Fit

The overall theme in having and maintaining this secret is "acting normal". Just because you have quit smoking does not mean you have to go around acting all weird. You may find this hard to believe but if you act calm you will feel calm. Protecting this secret will allow you to continue to act as if everything is fine. When you act like all is well you will feel well.

This is a no pity program. On my program you can not walk around displaying your withdrawal problem on your sleeve. Once again, you got yourself into this mess. Now you must be mature and act like a responsible adult. You do not get to have any pity. The mature thing to do is to be discrete about your predicament. When you started smoking, did you go around telling everyone? No, probably not. Did you keep it a secret? Well, look at this as another fun time to keep a secret.

Complaining about not being able to have a smoke because you're quitting is acting badly. Complaining is going to increase the feeling of withdrawal. If you continue to bicker about the situation you will be having a nicotine fit. "What happens when a child has a fit"? A fit is nothing more than acting badly. When you vow to act calm in your new life as a nonsmoker you will indeed be eliminating a great deal of the "nicotine fit", perhaps, even more than 75%. The withdrawal you experience after quitting is indeed an uncomfortable feeling. Knowing that it will soon pass and acting calmly will ease the discomfort immensely. Also, in the grand scheme of things, the withdrawal you will experience is not going to hospitalize you. Yes, we all know it is uncomfortable. So is having to go to the bathroom really bad. Your best line of defense is to be aware, be discreet, be confident, be prepared and get ready. When you are, hang on and *"Go For It" (quietly) Shhhhh.*

My story

It took him three months to notice. I'll call him Justin. Justin always gave me a hard time about smoking. Every time I saw this person instead of being frustrated about not smoking I was amused that he did not notice. It was my second day off smokes. We had made arrangements to go for lunch. The hostess sat us in a booth and gave us menus to look at. (There's no nonsmoking section) A couple of minutes later (felt like forever) the waitress came by and asked us if we wanted coffee. I abruptly replied "YES PLEASE"! I had a large grin on my face as I realized I had to protect my secret. I then put my stale gum in the ashtray. Justin asked me if everything was OK. My answer was, "Sure, everything is fine". I was smiling. I then began to relax and enjoyed the fact that he had not noticed. I thought putting the gum in the ashtray was a dead give-a-way. After lunch I was fidgeting and was a bit restless. Again Justin asked me if everything was all right. I smiled and blamed it on the coffee. I did not see Justin every day, but it did take him a long time to figure it out. He also thought it was funny that he had not noticed. To this day he still can not believe that I actually quit.

What do you tell them if they figure it out right away? Tell inquiring minds that you have just cut down. That's right, LIE! At this point, if they do figure it out, it is not beneficial that they know the truth. If they do, you may be tempted to seek sympathy and therefore increase your withdrawal symptoms which could lead to nicotine "fits".

Do you think you might be the exception and can honestly say you will seek no sympathy? Well consider then that a person who is quitting smoking could use their withdrawal episodes as a really good excuse to be "bitchy" or to be angry, bossy or irritable. They say misery loves company. Could it mean that acting this out would bring everyone down? Are you one of those people who wants it bad for everyone around you so you will not be the only one having a bad day? God I hope not. That wouldn't be right.

If this sounds like you, make a vow to do it differently. Do this on your own, all by yourself. It's your mess! Be a responsible adult and clean it up quietly. Be brave, and **"go for it"**.

Review

1. Remember to put some thought into choosing the right person to share your secret with.
2. Trade. Have a secret instead of a smoke.
3. Do not waste time and energy explaining yourself.
4. Protecting this secret will be fun.
5. Act normal! Stay calm, feel calm.
6. Seek no pity. Don't beg for sympathy.
7. Having a plan in place for when you are ready to "go for it" will create anticipation instead of dread. You are prepared!

Telling anyone your quitting creates unnecessary pressure for you. This is a private time for yourself. Be calm and discrete, act like an adult and just do it! Be strong my friend!

The bottom line:

Having this secret...
will get you through the difficult times.

How to Create Willpower

It is understandable that people have negative feelings towards quitting the nasty habit. Not surprising, the result of this is to procrastinate. Heck, even the idea of quitting could cause you to light up. All of this happens because you do not have the will power to quit. This program is designed to create will power.

Everything you have read in this book up to this point is all about developing will power. Willpower wasn't something I had. Willpower is something I developed. If you do all the work in this manual, you too can and will develop willpower!

> **Let's go over everything and see
> how your willpower is growing.**

1. The simple decision to alternate brands and to exercise the discipline it takes to do this faithfully is increasing your willpower.
2. Every time you smoke a cigarette other than your old brand you are confirming your decision to quit someday. Therefore, you are growing willpower.
3. When you tell people you are going to quit some day, you are growing willpower.
4. Smoking ultra-light cigarettes conjures up this mysterious power.
5. Doing the exercises and reading them (knowing them) definitely creates willpower.
6. Referring to this problem as a habit and not an addiction creates a mental picture, causing willpower. LIE! (More on this topic latter on.)
7. Combining the power of 1 to 6 creates a synergy that promotes unstoppable willpower.

Synergy is when 100+100=300
Synergy is powerful

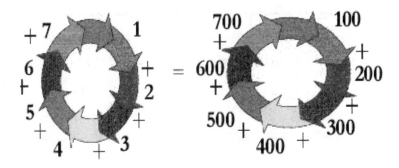

possible 1+1 could equal 3? To explain what this means picture a man and a woman together. If they combine themselves they can create a third person. Man + woman = baby (3).

The things you are being asked to do in this book are weak on their own. When you do them all together you have the recipe for creating a very powerful thing. This powerful thing will grow inside of you. You will feel it! Staying dedicated to the plan creates momentum.

This is the start of the mental propulsion mentioned earlier. I can remember this feeling like it was yesterday. It is a surge of mental power that can face anything!

Don't fool yourself. You too can have this power. Don't underestimate yourself either. Tap into yourself, do the work in this manual and feel it grow.

Will power is...Power!
because in order to have it you must
overpower your own mind

You have a strong mind. *This program is designed to reshape it.* When your mind becomes reshaped it will in fact be stronger than the old one. When this shaping takes place **you can** overpower your old self.

> # When you are willing to change,
> ## you are willing to reshape your thinking.
> ## When you do this,
> ## you will want to quit smoking.

When you can get to the point of saying, "Yes, I want to quit." You will get a surge of will power. Try it. Say it out loud, **"YES, I WANT TO QUIT SMOKING!"** Now say, **"I WANT TO BE A NONSMOKER!"** Did it feel like you meant it? If it did not, then go back and look at the quality of the exercises you have done. You did do the exercises, I hope.

Don't worry if it doesn't feel right, there is more work to do. Congratulations for coming this far. Keep going there is still plenty to do.

Exercise 5a

In order to reshape your thinking you need to know what it is you are currently thinking. Answer the following questions. (On paper)

♦ Why do you smoke?
♦ Why did you start?
♦ Are you still smoking for the same reasons you started?
♦ What has changed since then?
♦ Are you able to "see" the part that is the habit?
♦ Are you able to recognize the addictive part?
Write your answers in the form of a short paragraph.

Exercise 5b

Write another short paragraph explaining how you feel about quitting. List your fears and your concerns. Write exactly what bothers you about quitting. List your reasons for feeling this way? Your reasons are very important to make a note of. It is most important to write this information down.

Have you ever said, *"Why should I quit? I'm going to die any way."* How about,

- ◆ I'm afraid I'll fail.
- ◆ It's too hard.

- ◆ I enjoy smoking.
- ◆ I don't care

Acknowledge all your thoughts no matter how negative they are.

What is your primary motivation for quitting? Is it health, money, image or a combination? What will you mostly focus on when you open your last pack?

You need to know this "stuff" so put down the book and go to work. Take a trip inside of yourself. It beats going to the morgue!

Will power being developed

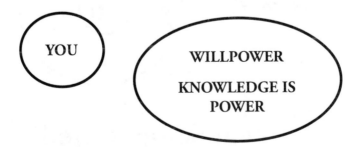

Willpower in progress.

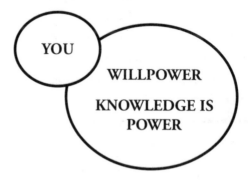

The smaller self does not completely want to quit smoking.

**When you become a bigger person...
you can do big things.**

Your new and improved self has a surge of power and knows it can quit smoking. At this point you feel like there isn't anything you can't do!

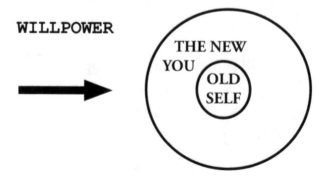

You are empowered!

Reshaping

You are well on your way if you can say out-loud, "I am willing to change." Try saying, "I want to change! I want to change now!" Go on, give it a try. See how it feels. What do you have to lose? You have a whole NEW WORLD to gain. Right now all you have to do is be willing. If you are willing it will mean you are doing the exercises in this book.

I am bringing it up again because in this segment and the one to follow there is more work to do. It is all geared towards reshaping. So let's go.

Do you know which beliefs keep you smoking? Let's use this example—I enjoy smoking. This is a destructive belief system that will keep you smoking. Search your mind for what you believe about your justifications for smoking.

Exercise 6

Write down your six top destructive beliefs. Include, I am addicted. This is a very powerful list, and I will show you how to change it to one that will empower you. Put down the book and do this now.

Now look at your list and ask yourself what your beliefs are costing you. (Other than money.) Are you able to see how your beliefs are hurting you? Can you see that it is those beliefs that keep you smoking?

Examples of destructive thoughts-

♦ I'm young and my health is not in jeopardy as I haven't been smoking for that long.
♦ Smoking is a good stress reliever.
♦ I enjoy smoking.
♦ Smoking passes the time.
♦ I gave up everything else. I won't give up my smokes.
♦ I am too old, why bother?

Is it really worth hanging on to beliefs like these? Can you see how they are hurting you?

The caterpillar did not want to change. But he did anyway. His life depended on it. When the transformation was complete he broke out of his cocoon and he could fly! He was very excited and happy he made the change.

When you open your last pack see yourself in a cocoon and take some time out of the everyday life to look after yourself.

You have faced other challenges and adversity. You can do this too!

Take Back Your Control

Consider for a moment that it was not you who did the last exercise. What if that was just the addiction talking? Could your addiction be making you think those thoughts. Wouldn't that be convenient? Then it could have you smoke forever.

What you need to do now is find a way to see how those beliefs are ruling your life. Look at what those beliefs are costing you. I am not just talking about the money. You must get angry with them! Look at how much control they have on you. Wouldn't you like to take the control back? You can. Get angry at the negative beliefs and say, "This must change! I can change it! This must change now!"

Earlier you made a list of your reasons for wishing to be a nonsmoker. Look at this list and search for the common theme. (pg 26) **What is it on this list that is your main motivation?** It is even better if you have more than one. The more you have the better. This "thing" that will motivate you will also help eliminate your negative thoughts.

Say it again, "This must change! I can change it! This must change now"! It feels good to take control, doesn't it?

Think of yourself as the captain of your ship. You have just changed course. Congratulations.

Beliefs Impact Our Lives

(Q) *What is a belief?*
(A) A belief is a feeling of certainty about what something means.
There are three levels of certainty-
1. **Opinion**
2. **Belief**
3. **Conviction**

Think back to when you started smoking. The reasons why you started are your belief system. What did you think smoking would mean? What did you think smoking would do? Did you think smoking would get you something? *Your thinking is what made you light up.*

Whatever your thoughts were back then, ask yourself, "Are you smoking for the same reasons today?"

Are you using references from the past to support what you believe today?

Nothing in life has any meaning, except the meaning we give it.

(Q) *What is the purpose of a belief?*
(A) It is a guide in making decisions. Every decision you make is about gaining pleasure or avoiding pain.

Think about the pain that is usually associated with quitting. **Yikes!** So, at some level, you decide not to quit, thus avoiding pain.

When you started smoking, what you thought smoking would mean created pleasure.

Procrastination means to avoid pain!

The decisions we make impact our lives as well as others.

DESTRUCTIVE EMPOWERING

Ted Bundy	Mother Theresa
Hitler	Martin Luther King

Change your beliefs. Change your life.

By looking at this chart you can see how your beliefs shape your life. Can you also see the power they have?

Quitting smoking is not hard.
Stopping what you think is!

One way to stop what we think is to question it. Check all your thoughts to see if they are worth keeping.

Replacing Limiting Beliefs

In order to replace your negative beliefs you must be very clear as to what they are. Look at the list you made earlier. (Review page 45)

Exercise 7

For each thought listed ask, *"What is silly, ridiculous or stupid about it?"* Come up with as many answers as possible. Then ask, *"What is hanging onto this belief costing me or how is this belief hurting me?"* Also ask, *"What will this cost me in the future if I don't change it?"* Make your answers read like a paragraph. Another important and necessary part of this step is to include, as much as possible, negative emotional pain. **FEEL IT!**

The purpose of this exercise is to destabilize your old beliefs. You can do this by questioning them. Are you certain you want to keep them? By asking the questions mentioned above you shake your certainty; therefore making it easier to let go of them. Once you're ready to let go of them you can then start to build new and empowering beliefs.

As I mentioned earlier it is harder to hang onto things that cause us pain. Think of a time you were in a bad relationship. The more emotional pain you feel the easier it is to end it, right? How could you walk away from a relationship that is going well? You have a relationship with your cigarettes. You need to see and feel the pain it is causing, in order to **"let it go"**.

By examining your beliefs and questioning them you are rocking the foundation and creating a new base for new and empowering beliefs that will change everything. With these new beliefs in place quitting will be easier than you could ever imagine. The brain naturally wants to move away from pain and towards pleasure.

The exercise you did on creating reasons to be a nonsmoker is where you will find this pleasure. (Review page 26 & 30) In the end what you are doing is changing your view of smoking to being painful and your view of being a nonsmoker to pleasurable. In the long and the short of things you need to **think of what pleasure you are going to get, and attach pain to what you are leaving behind!**

**Transformations occur with
the changing of a belief.**

We can consciously decide what we are going to believe.

It sounds so simple but to change a belief you just have to make a decision and do it. Just say, "I do not believe that anymore!" Go ahead, get angry with those out-dated, useless beliefs. Kick them out the door!

Destructive	Empowering
I'm too old to quit .	I will feel happy when I quit.
I enjoy smoking.	I don't enjoy smoking now.
It relaxes me.	I can relax on my own.

**Do this with your list of old
out-dated beliefs.**

Interrupting Habitual Thoughts

When you have thought something to be true for a long time and you try to change it you may find that you are thinking things habitually. What this means is, even though you are no longer believing your old thoughts, they have a tendency to creep back in. There is a way to stop this from occurring. You must, however, do some brain-storming to interrupt this habitual thought pattern. Don't worry. It's not as difficult as it sounds. Put the time in and sit down and put on your thinking cap. I can and will give you some examples in the following exercise, but YOU must come up with interruptions that you know will have *MEANING* for *YOU*.

Tony Robbins the mastermind behind personal change calls this interruption "scratching". I have done several personal changes using this system and can vouch for its merits. I had this system in place when I quit smoking. I didn't know there was a formula that was designed to help people plan their changes. There is a formula and it works.

Exercise 8
Scratching out old thoughts
Right down your recurring thoughts you want gone. Or is it a feeling that keeps coming back?

Example
The thought of opening your last pack automatically creates fear. This is a thought with fear attached to it.

Thought: Scared of opening my last pack.
The scratch: I am opening a Christmas present. I know quitting
smoking will be like a gift. This gift is a new life.
I am so excited about being a nonsmoker!

Habitual thought	The scratch	New thought
What does it mean	Interruption thought	New meaning
Fear	Christmas is great	Quitting is a gift

For many people this is the hardest exercise. Mostly
this is because of the time it takes to come up with thought
interruptions that will really work for you. The way to do this
successfully is to create thoughts that will make you *feel good*
and that you know you can remember. You must do this process
for every thought you want to replace.

I would like to give you an unrelated example of a
time when I used Tony's system of what I call, "Deliberate
Change"

There was a time in my life when I found it very hard
to initiate conversation with strangers. It always bothered me
that people didn't talk to me. It occurred to me that I didn't talk
either. I would see the same people in the gym every other day.
One year later neither of us would even say hi! I was so curious
about how this happens. We go about our business keeping our
thoughts to ourselves day in and day out. I wondered if we do
it because in our culture we are taught not to talk to strangers.
It could be the reason. I don't really know.

I thought if that is true, the rule was meant for young
children. I am an adult now and just because they don't talk to
me doesn't mean I can't talk to them.

My new thought was to go out and just say, "Hi." It didn't matter how much I wanted to say hi, I would just forget, as it was a life-style I had become used to for over twenty years. When I would remember to say hi, I would well up with all this fear. Oh great, now I have this fear to deal with.

How do you make the fear go away? I thought I would just muster up the courage and become brave. I was brave but the fear was still inside. I thought this would go away eventually. What I was doing was forcing myself. Being the first person to initiate conversation was really hard. I was struggling with it every day. I figured the reason people don't talk to one another is because everyone has these fears! I continued on, thinking it was like a muscle. Once you got used to using it, it would become easier. It never did.

I have always been interested in personal growth. One day someone asked me if I was interested in listening to Tony Robbins' tapes on Personal Power. I was very excited, as I'd seen him on TV. So just like you I had to do the above exercises. Just a different subject. Here is what I did:

1   Fear of talking to strangers

2   The interruption-
    (a) I would think of my family and my closest friends who are out of town. I would feel how much I miss them.
    (b) I am smiling as I picture my best friend, who lives a long ways away, opening my Christmas gift.
    (c) I think of my distant relatives and I wish I knew them better.
    (d) Deep down inside we are all related to one another.

3 New thoughts

(a) *When I see a stranger* I picture them on Christmas day. They are happy and filled with joy.

(b) I am missing an opportunity to get to know them.

(c) *When I see a stranger* I think of them as a distant relative. Older men are my grandpas; middle-aged men are my uncles; young women are my cousins and so on.

| Fear | Family/friends | Comfortable |

When the fear creeps in, I push it back out with the new thoughts. My new thoughts work for me because they have special meaning to me.

I am no longer afraid to approach strangers.

You must do this exercise for every thought you would like to kick out of your life. It is very tedious but well worth the time and effort. My whole world has changed because I find it so easy to approach people. I do not even think of them as strangers anymore. I see them as "family". The old fears are completely gone! You can use this formula for any thing you want to feel differently about. Go ahead! There's a whole new world waiting for you!

Pain vs. Pleasure

When you write the old thoughts attach as much pain as you can. If you can't write it down then feel it when you think it. A sure way to create pain is to consider what will happen down the road if you're STILL smoking and hanging on to those crummy thoughts? (Review pg 24 exercise 3a.)

When you write the list of your new way of thinking make it as pleasurable as possible.

Exercise 9b

In your mind go back and forth with the two thoughts. Feel the pain-feel the pleasure. Feel the pain-feel the pleasure. Do this for five minutes with each item on your list.

As stated earlier, your mind will automatically move towards pleasure and away from pain. What you are doing in these exercises is creating pain and attaching it to your old thoughts. *You then need to create new thoughts and attach pleasure to them.* Your brain will do the rest as it will automatically reject the painful thoughts and adopt the pleasurable ones. Poof! You just changed!

If you have a difficult time with this you must work on creating pain and creating pleasure. This is the key. Review pages 25, 26 & 30.

Take a Break

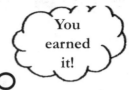

You have done a great deal of work up to this point. Congratulations for being so willing to change.

The hardest part is over; you know, living through all that pain. Thank-you for being such a willing participant.

Before we go on I would like to share a personal view on the subject of people who are being stubborn about their habit.

I call it the Comparison

The Teenager

Jimmy gets a three wheeler motor bike for his birthday. After handing him the keys, his parents make him promise to always wear a helmet and never, ever drink and drive! "Yeah sure, Mom, Dad, thank you so much!"

Off Jimmy goes to get his girlfriend and a case of beer. Leaving the empty beer cans behind and forgetting his helmet they go off for a fun ride in the woods.

Jimmy's parent gets a call from the hospital emergency room. Jimmy's mom cries," Why didn't he listen to us?"

The End, or is it?

The Smoker

The Canadian Lung Association,
The Cancer Society, doctors, Yule Brynner and
countless other people know smoking is killing
thousands of people every year.
They are reaching out with life saving
information!

Are you going to listen?

Please do not be like the teenager who thinks he is invincible.

You didn't listen in the past.

Listen to me now!

Smoking can kill you!

The Choices You Make

Consider this still a break, as you don't need a pen in your hand. I need to take you on a journey. I hope you will follow me.

Here we go. Find a comfortable place to sit, or lay down if you like, as long as you are able to relax. After you read the following, close your eyes and recall the story.

You have been smoking for too long. You have developed a very bad smoker's cough. The coughing scares you. One day you are coughing and you spit out blood! Now you're more scared than ever. Right away you call the doctor to make an appointment. You're frustrated because he can not see you until Friday. You have to wait for three days! You hate waiting. This is even worse because you're scared too. As the days pass your cough continues. You see the blood every now and again. Each time you become more scared. Your worst fear is cancer.

Friday comes about and you find yourself in the waiting room waiting! There is nothing you would like to do more than run for the door and have the problem just go away. You know you're in trouble. While you sit there you contemplate quitting smoking. A big part of you wishes you had quit ages ago.

The doctor is examining your lungs. Breathe in, breathe out. Again and again he says it. You know he is going to give you a lecture on smoking. Naturally, he urges you to quit. He tells you to get some blood work done at the lab and also you need to get x-rays. "It is urgent," he tells you, "Get it done today!"

He did not relieve any of your fears; in fact he only made them worse. You can't remember the last time you were this scared. You rush over to the lab, tear off to get the x-rays and can't wait to get back home. Once there you sit back, relax and light up a smoke. You feel stupid sitting there with a smoke in your hand. You realize you need to wait for the test results to come in. You know it is going to be a crummy weekend. You sit there wishing you had already quit smoking.

You continue to smoke, cough and spit up blood. You live with the constant worry in the back of your mind. Wednesday the doctor's office calls and schedules you in for the very next day.

When you arrive they immediately put you in his private office. You have a bad feeling about this one. He is looking at your file. He looks up at you, then looks back at your file. He's not saying anything. He is just looking and clicking his pen up and down.

You start to feel like you're going pale. You know it's bad. The doctor looks up and confirms it. There is no easy way to tell you that you have inoperable lung cancer. The damage is too advanced. Your lungs are in such a mess even radiation will not help. This cancer spread extraordinarily fast.

He sounds sympathetic as he says he is sorry and wishes there were something he could do. You ask him, "How long do I have?" Six months if you're lucky. You slump down in your chair and turn three shades lighter. All of your energy just left your body. You are in shock! You can not believe this could happen to you. This kind of thing only happens to other people! You're overwhelmed with wishing you had quit smoking a long time ago. In your mind you're thinking, "God, I wish I had quit smoking two years ago. Why didn't I quit two years ago?"

The doctor nudges you and asks if there is someone he can call to come and get you. He recommends you not be alone. You give him your best friend's number and go back into your state of wishing you had quit. Over and over you think quietly "Why?... Why?... Why?... Why didn't I quit!" You are trapped in your overwhelming feeling of regret! You desperately wish you could turn back the time. If you could you know you would do things differently. God! If only you could go back!

> ## *Exercise 10*
> Now it's your turn. Are you comfortable? Read the story until you feel you know it well enough to recall it and the feelings that go with it. Feel what this would be like if it were really true. Imagine for a moment this will actually happen to you. See the doctor telling you that you have six months to live. This exercise is called visualization. There is another part to this exercise. I will share it with you shortly, but first you must do the visualization.

> ## You know smoking will lead to certain doom.

See if you can't imagine what it would be like to live with permanent regret.

The above story you just read is available in DVD

This is how it came to be:
This book is a one day workshop.
The one day workshop was turned into a Home Study Edition
The DVD The Choices You Make comes with the Home Study Edition.

The DVD is never sold separate due to being taken out of context to the BMP Method.

PROGRAM ONE
(Pleasure)

This is an old program running.
You installed it at the time you started smoking.

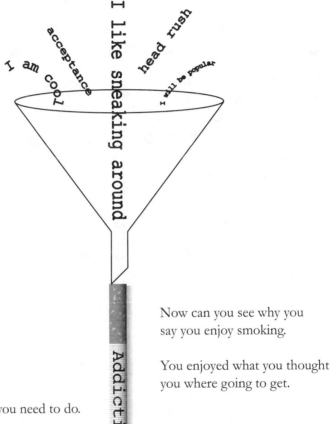

Now can you see why you
say you enjoy smoking.

You enjoyed what you thought
you where going to get.

Three things you need to do.

1) Be aware of your reasons
(meaning) for starting smoking .
(Programming)
2a) See if it is still true today. If not delete this program it has been
running in the back of your mind.
2b) If some reasons are still true decide right now it is time to believe
something new.
3) Create new beliefs... yes! Just like that.

PROGRAM TWO

(Pain)

This program is also running in the present moment and
goes hand in hand to keeping your original reasons for
starting smoking in tact.

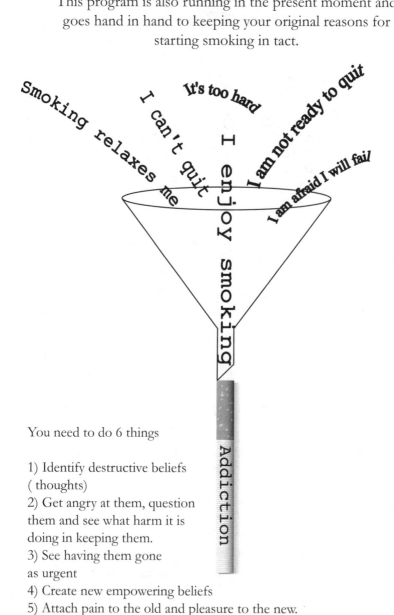

You need to do 6 things

1) Identify destructive beliefs
(thoughts)
2) Get angry at them, question
them and see what harm it is
doing in keeping them.
3) See having them gone
as urgent
4) Create new empowering beliefs
5) Attach pain to the old and pleasure to the new.
6) see pg 25 and 30

A NEW BEGINNING
What does continuing smoking mean now?

(Pain)

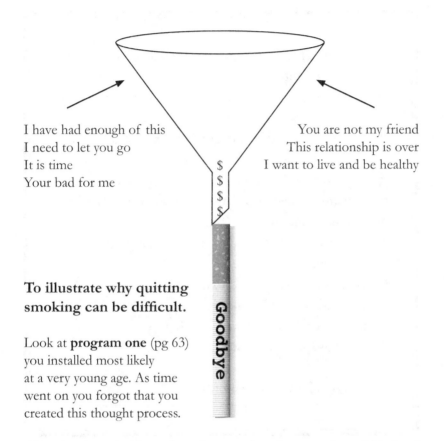

I have had enough of this
I need to let you go
It is time
Your bad for me

You are not my friend
This relationship is over
I want to live and be healthy

To illustrate why quitting smoking can be difficult.

Look at **program one** (pg 63) you installed most likely at a very young age. As time went on you forgot that you created this thought process.

Years later you decide you're going to quit and you run into all kinds of problems; largely due to the original meaning you created. Each time you try to quit and fail it reinforces the notion that quitting is too hard.

These two systems running at the same time creates massive conflict for the brain. In order to quit with less strife is to understand the importance of going back to the original reasons for starting and uninstall this reasoning (program).

Once you do this and other parts of the BMP Method **program two** (pg 64) the disempowering thinking will no longer be true.

Part two summary

- Remember the reasons why you will not tell people you have quit.
- Doing this program creates an unstoppable surge of energy called synergy.
- You have tapped into your destructive beliefs which are keeping your addiction in place.
- You now understand how will power is made.
- You are aware of how your beliefs control your life.
- Change your beliefs - Change your life.
- Transformations occur with the changing of a belief.
- You can interrupt habitual thinking.
- The old way of thinking has pain attached to it. The new way makes you feel happy.)
- You have imagined living with dread.

Feeling like a new person yet?

Part Three

YOUR MIND IS LIKE A COMPUTER

Toss Out The Old Program
Bring in the new one!

Tap into the Subconscious

> **Quiz:** What is the hardest part of quitting smoking?
>
> What is the second hardest part?
>
> **Stay tuned.**
> **These questions will be answered shortly.**

You can relax now.
You have gone through the hardest part.

What year is it? Remember the visualization (pg 60)? Well, I have good news. You are not going to die. That journey I took you on took place two years into the future! Come back to the present moment and feel like you were given that second chance. It is not too late! You can avoid all that stuff! You just took a trip into the future. Take the knowledge and apply it today!

Please do not wait too long.

By now you should be feeling excited and confident about quitting. You have done a great deal of work. I hope you are feeling proud of yourself for realizing you had to change. I hope you reward yourself by doing something special.

This next part of the plan is designed to help you remember all the important things we have covered. You will learn how to tap into the subconscious. If you do this step there is no way you could forget anything! What good are all those exercises if you can't remember them?

This next step is also going to help you to relax. More importantly it will help you learn to relax as a nonsmoker. At the end of this segment I will also give you my special formula for dealing with the last pack.

Are Your Exercises Completed ?

You now need all of the exercises that you have been asked to do. Check the boxes of the exercises you have completed.

Part one

Exercise 1 pg 22 ☐   Exercise 2 pg 23 ☐

Exercise 3a pg 25 ☐   Exercise 3b pg 26 ☐

Exercise 4 pg 30 ☐

Part Two

Exercise 5a pg42 ☐   Exercise 5b pg 43 ☐

Exercise 6 pg 45 ☐   Exercise 7 pg 50 ☐

Exercise 8 pg 52 ☐   Exercise 9a pg 56 ☐

Exercise 9b pg 56 ☐   Exercise 10 pg 62 ☐

Part Three
Implementing all exercises.

All the above exercises will help you to record your tailor made program in a story format. The next part will explain how to make your program. Keep reading because there is more work to do.

Keep Going...You're almost done!

A New Program: A New Life

Most important to remember about my plan is that each step is rather simple. However when they are combined with each other you get a very powerful synergy! I must stress this because this next step is equally important and should not be overlooked.

What you must do is go and purchase a sixty or ninety- minute tape for recording valuable information. This information will come from the exercises you have done. It is not recommended you record over an existing tape, as the quality of sound is not as good. You will be making this tape and will be listening to it often. I would like you to have quality in mind. This will make your listening experience more enjoyable. Now that we have covered all that, lets go!

Gather all your exercises and put them in order. I am going to show you how to custom design your program. I am sure by this point you realize you will be using *your voice*. This is just as important as the content of your tape.

This is deliberately designed so you will be talking to you!

Have you ever had a dream and it seemed so real?

> **The subconscious does not know the difference between the truth and a lie.**

The reason is because the mind in that state can not tell the difference. The same thing is true when you are in a very relaxed state of mind. I will explain how you do it in a moment. It's not complicated, so don't worry. But first, take in a deep breath (*yes now*) and exhale. Do that a couple of times. Try it again and pretend you are taking a puff off a smoke.

Many people think that smoking relaxes them. There are two things to consider:

1 When you smoke you are actually taking in a deep breath, exhaling, taking in a deep breath and exhaling. Little do smokers know they are doing deep breathing exercises. This is, in fact, what is making them feel so relaxed. This is why I asked you to try it and pretend you are smoking.

2 Is it not a coincidence that when smokers take a "smoke break" it is about fifteen minutes? Well isn't that a good excuse to take a fifteen minute break?

Taking a "break" and deep breathing, yes that would be relaxing. My point is that *you can still do those things without the smoke.* One sure way is to allow yourself that "time out" even as a nonsmoker, especially when you're a fresh nonsmoker.

Now you know, it is deep breathing that relaxes you. Allow yourself some time to relax and listen to your recording you are about to make. OK? Let's get cracking!

Think of your mind like a computer. The audio I am going to show you how to make is the "disk". When you insert the disk into yourself you will be inserting (listening to) all that you want to be real. All that you want to be true. This is a good time to tell lies. Go ahead and make them up. On (page 40) I said I would explain more on how the lie is related to will power. The mind will not know it is a lie.

It does a great deal of good to refer to this problem as a habit and not an addiction. Having this view is good for your will power, as it will feel more manageable. Some good lies may include:

♥ I never really enjoyed smoking.

♥ It was just something to do.

♥ The smell of others' cigarettes will not bother me.

Whatever you want to be true, including your new beliefs, is what you have written down. You need to be prepared to record. Have everything in place for when you hit the record button. Be ready to run through it without stopping.

Key steps in preparing to record
(examples will follow)

The beginning

- ♥ You must use your own voice.
- ♥ Use a slow and relaxed, quiet tone of voice.
- ♥ Introduce yourself and state your purpose.
- ♥ Acknowledge your voice as the gospel truth.
- ♥ Do some deep breathing exercises and become very relaxed.
- ♥ Your mind and body must be relaxed and comfortable.
- ♥ Take yourself down to a deep level of relaxation.
- ♥ Then make yourself go down even deeper.
- ♥ Take 10 - 15 minutes to get into this state
- ♥ With you mind's eye look around. See your power.

The body:
Part one (You will need)

- ♥ Your list of reasons for why you want to be a non-smoker, (positive format)
- ♥ Your list of the things you know you must avoid,
- ♥ Your list of your obstacles that you are prepared to face and challenge,
- ♥ Statements that make real what you want real, (Lie)

♥ Statements of your new beliefs,
♥ To admit and prepare for the challenge,
♥ To remind yourself how relaxed you are,
♥ To refer to your power that you now recognize,
♥ To talk about embracing this power,
♥ To be ready to listen to your power,
♥ To feel strong,
♥ To remind yourself you speak only the truth.

Intermission

Find a mellow piece of music that you know will inspire you. Insert about 90 seconds of it, or leave 40 seconds of silence.

Part two

♥ Repeat part one mixing up the order of the statements.
♥ The key to your program is to be relaxed and repetitive.
♥ There is no wrong way to present this information.

Intermission

Choose another mellow piece of music that you know will inspire you.   Insert about 90 seconds of it, or leave 40 seconds of silence.

Part three

Repeat part one. Mix the order up again

Part four

Use the left over tape with more inspiring music. End your tape with *I QUIT!*

Self - Programming Continued

To insure you have a great personal audio, I am including an exact transcript of the one I made. I want to insure you are able to duplicate the format. If you are having any problems you can use mine as a reference. I also do not mind if you borrow all or part of my personal tape for your personal use only.

Please note it was many years ago when I made my audio. I used a tape deck. You may have new options available to you. Any time you see the word tape it is meant as "audio". Whatever you use it should be something that you can play back and no one else will hear but you.

Lets go over key points for making a great recording-

The beginning

1   The tone of voice is soft and hypnotic - Pretend you are Ravine or Romaine. They are masters at hypnosis. Yes you may feel silly. It is a good idea to practice recording your voice. Think of it as a dress rehearsal. Remember how important what you are doing is. Allow yourself to go ahead and feel silly. Heck, have fun. You're making a new life!

2   The introduction is your name and refer to yourself as the truth and nothing but the truth. Also for all intent and purpose this tape will help you to quit smoking.

3   Use a count down for taking yourself deeper and deeper.

4   **Your power is the new you.** Go ahead. Look at your shiny new self. Embrace it as your **"power"**.

5   Once you reach your deepest level of relaxing you may start to talk more in sentences. Tell yourself what you need to remember.

The body

Part one (sample statements)
Reasons for quitting:
In this segment you may refer to the negative aspect of why you are quitting, as well as the positive aspects. Don't leave anything out. **It is all important.**
- ♥ I do not like the stains on my fingers.
- ♥ My clothes will not stink anymore.
- ♥ Smoking is a filthy disgusting habit.
- ♥ I will save tons of money.
- ♥ Etcetera, etc.

Things to avoid
When do you habitually light up? What causes you stress? Is there a person you need to avoid? Put some thought into this.
- ♥ I am going to avoid talking on the phone.
- ♥ I will go for a walk instead of hanging out in the coffee room at work.
- ♥ I am not going to drink alcohol for two or three weeks.

Recognize and acknowledge the challenge you are embracing. This will be hard at times but you know you can handle it.

Include comments that will build your confidence. (You know what will bring you confidence.)
- ♥ I have the power to break the chains of tar and nicotine.
- ♥ I can see myself living as a nonsmoker.
- ♥ I know I can do it!

By now you should have a lot of paper in front of you. Take the information in all your exercises and rewrite it in story format for your personal tape. Let's say you have ten items in each list. When you record, what you will do is mix things up. You do this by taking two or three items from each list. The idea is to mix things up so it does not sound like you are reading from a list.

Example:

I am so looking forward to being a nonsmoker... I am going to save so much money (pause). My fingers won't have ugly stains on them... I feel so strong with my new power. (Pause) I know I can lose this nasty, filthy habit. (Pause) I am not going to talk on the phone for more than five minutes... Instead of hanging out with the smokers at work, I am going to go for a walk. (pause)... And so on...

Intermissions

If you chose to use music as intermissions make sure the volume does not change too much. This is so you won't be jarred out of your relaxed state of mind. If you don't want to use music just have approximately one minute of silence.

Parts two and three

The reason for this interruption is so you can repeat what you just said but this time you will do it in a different order.

Your audio should be at least 30 minutes long.

If you are using the old technology like I did, you may use the other side of your tape to make a whole new program, including the part when you take yourself deep into a relaxed state or make a copy of side one.

Summary of main key factors

1   Your tone of voice is hypnotic and slow leaving about 5-10 seconds of air space every few sentences.
2   Realize the importance of getting completely relaxed. Take the time on your tape 10-15 minutes.
3   Make sure you are organized before you start.
4   Be repetitive.
5   Remind yourself your voice is the truth.
6   When you record make sure there is no background noise or interruptions.
7   Say your name at least two times in your statements. (Barb, you know you can do this.)
8   The last thing on your audio will be **I QUIT**. Then leave the rest blank.

This recording must be made before you open your last pack.

~

You will listen to your audio while you are on your last pack.

Turn to page 95 for the contents of my audio. (Verbatim)

When I was on my last pack, I listened to my program once or twice a day. When I was finished my last pack I used it three or four times a day for about six weeks. To this day I do not remember what part of my tape was a lie! It all became true for me. The only thing I remember is I used to say I enjoyed smoking. However that girl is long gone! My tape helped me to become a new and better person. I sure hope you make a good recording and become the person you know you want to be.

Remember the quiz?

Q. What is the hardest part of
   quitting smoking?
A. Getting to the point of making the
   decision.

Q. What is the second hardest part?
A. Remembering! You made the decision.

This recording is going to help you remember all the work you have done in this book. This is why you need to play it over and over again. You have done a great deal of work. When you have quit you will not have to THINK about the things we have covered in this book. All you have to do is push PLAY! You are the computer. The audio is the disk containing everything you need to know. All you have to do is listen!

Put in the time and effort in making a
good quality recording and quitting
will be easier than ever!

Breaking the Chains

Wow, you have come a long way! Can you feel the anticipation of the "Jump"? Before I share my special formula for dealing with your last pack, I would like you to know how it feels to break the chains of tar and nicotine.

You may already know this feeling if you have quit before. In this case recall those feelings and focus on how wonderful it felt. It is a huge reminder that quitting can be a great experience.

For those of you who have not ever quit before I wish you could believe me when I tell you it is like breaking out of prison! You do not fully understand the hold smoking has on you until you break away. When you do finally burst out it is an overwhelming feeling of control. Having this kind of control makes you feel like there is not anything you can't accomplish. This feeling of accomplishment is so wonderful! One day I was walking to the store and on my way there the feeling of accomplishment came over me. I thought to myself, "Wow! I really did it!" I smiled big and a wave of goose bumps came over me. A wave of freedom!

My addiction was just as strong as the one you carry. I smoked a pack and a half a day. I faced the same challenge you will face. I tell you, if I can quit this nasty thing that plagues our world so can you. I struggled with it for thirteen years before I finally got it right. Many people still can't believe I quit!

> ## Do keep in mind…
> ## OVERCOMING THIS CHALLENGE
> ## IS POSSIBLE!
> ### You too can do it! Go for it!

The Mathematical Equation to Freedom

When you get that "feeling", the one we discussed on page seventeen see if you can't hold onto to it until the following Monday. If you have "it" and you just can't wait any longer then go ahead... Jump! If you can hold on, unleash this surge of power on a Monday. As a matter of fact being ready and holding on a little while longer can give you an extra surge of power. This is because by this point you can't stand smoking any longer. Hanging on for a couple of more days will make you even more determined to lose the nasty thing. It may help you in your planning if every Friday, Saturday and Sunday you tune in to your environment, and current life's stress and ask yourself if you "feel" ready.

The time has arrived. Feel excited, happy and proud of yourself. Give yourself credit for being willing to take this leap. Put away all your ashtrays Sunday night. Get rid of your existing pack of smokes so that on Monday you will be opening a brand new small pack. (A package of 20 and not your old brand!)

On page twenty three you were working on eliminating the habitual cigarettes. Your goal was to get to the point of being able to go for four hours in the morning without a smoke. Congratulations if you did this. If you did not it will be required now. When you wake up go and get your smokes. Open the pack, and **write on the inside flap: Last pack (your name).** Then put them out of sight until later.

You must not light up your first cigarette on Monday until you have been awake for four hours exactly. Your next smoke will be four hours after the time you butt-out the first one. You will smoke only four cigarettes each day for five days.

There is another very important factor to consider when you smoke these cigarettes.

You must sit alone whenever possible. You must not have any music or TV. Do not talk on the phone or sit by the computer. You must do NOTHING! Just sit there and smoke. Think of it as administering a drug. You are only smoking for the dose of tar and nicotine. Do not be surprised if you feel silly. Do not be surprised if it doesn't taste good. This is all part of the plan.

The mathematical equation
1:4 hrs for 5 days =20 $S + 2 S+1$ M *your done*
~ Saturday you can borrow 2
~ Sunday you can borrow 1
~ Monday you are done.

Before you go out for the day figure out how many cigarettes you will need to take with you. Do not take the whole pack! If you like you can leave your pack at home and take two smokes with you. Or you can leave your smokes at work and take whatever the amount adds up to, based on the time involved.

Keep busy. Do not sit around waiting for the clock to strike. Go out for a walk. Go to the library, read or work on a puzzle. Play your home made tape. Stay active and remember your secret you must protect. You know you can do this. Be strong and hang on. Think over and over to yourself, "I do not want to smoke any more. I do not want to smoke any more."

Do not argue about it. The answer is always, "I do not want to smoke! I want to be a nonsmoker! I want to be a nonsmoker!" I don't care if you have to say it a million times. Eventually your brain will remember.

More important rules to live by:

♥ Do not drink alcohol for at least two weeks. For all you party animals out there, this is not a whole lot to ask as two weeks is a very small amount of time in the grand scheme of things. Take time off and look after this thing you are dealing with. The parties will be there when you're done. No, not even one drink. Drinking will weaken you and promote an "I don't care" attitude. Just trust me on this one.

♥ Deliberately go out of your home without a pack of smokes. Return home just before your next one is due. Enjoy how it feels to walk out the door without them. You will like it.

♥ Avoid stress, stressed out people, bars, parties and smorgasbords!

♥ Be very careful of the snack food you chose to eat. Avoid peanuts and cheese if you are worried about weight gain.

♥ Remember if you can quit smoking you can do anything, including losing weight, if you must.

If you have ignored my pleas to complete these exercises, consider showing this book to your employer and they can decide to implement this method for all staff who smoke and I can assist you in a live workshop.

If you do not have employment or a supportive employer you can contact me directly to arrange to be in a group or a one-on-one session. bmpmethod@shaw.ca

It's Only Three Weeks

When you wake up the
following Monday, say out loud,

> **"I am a nonsmoker and I feel great!"**

Throughout the day you will be faced with uncomfortable moments. Moments you will go through quietly and calmly. Tell yourself that this uncomfortable feeling will pass. Tell yourself, "This is the price I pay for lighting up". If you have to, repeat those thoughts over and over again! Take responsibility for your actions and realize this discomfort is for a very short period of time in relation to how long you smoked and the rest of your life.

Simultaneously, *think of three weeks, then the rest of your life. Three weeks versus my whole life.* Tell yourself the price to pay for smoking all this time is 3 weeks!

> **You can live through that!**
> **Grit your teeth and just do it!**

Life will be smoother after three weeks. Keep listening to your recording. Get a audio player for when you are away from home. Use the audio player if there are people in your home you are keeping this secret from. Tell them you are meditating or something.

Your Thoughts Will Save You.

♥ I am a nonsmoker.

♥ I will pay the price for lighting up.

♥ Three weeks is a small price to pay.

♥ I do not want to smoke.

♥ I want to be a nonsmoker.

♥ This urge will pass.

♥ I have had worse headaches.

♥ I am strong; I can do it!

A thought that is repeated over and over is called a mantra. Take some time and come up with some that have special meaning for you.

I hope you have enjoyed the process of change. It involves work, but I hope you have fun with it and realize you are worth the time and effort.

I wish you all the best and...

Good luck!

Turning In

Have you ever heard someone say they were going to turn in for the night? Sleep is often referred to as turning in. What happens after sleep? Do you feel rested and rejuvenated? For the most part I believe people do. This feeling of being rested is a key to what happens when we turn in. Turning in is good for us.

You do not have to go to sleep in order to gain this energy. You can consciously turn in by doing all the work that I have provided for you in these pages. All of it is designed to get you to go within. Make it fun.

There is another way to turn in. Go and get a mirror. Look at your eyes very closely. Stare right into them. Focus on the words "The eyes are the windows to the soul." If the eyes were the windows to the soul, why wouldn't we look in our own? Try this and look in for about ten minutes. You may or may not like what you see. But hey, if you don't look how are you going to know what to improve on? When we improve ourselves we improve the quality of our lives. I swear it is worth the journey!

The answers are there inside of you not in the drugstore!

Not without humor
How I bug smokers in a fun way:

I am visiting with a friend; she lights up.
I say, "Can you hear that?" She says "What?"
"You can't hear that?" She looks at me funny....
I walk over to her... "That...You don't hear it?"
The usual response is, "I don't hear anything?"
I put my ears up to her chest and say, "It's your
lungs, they're crying, HELP ME...HELP ME..."
I tell them I can hear it....
I wonder if they will think about it later when they are
alone?

My other favorite one:
*I am standing outside, waiting for something
or someone.*

To pass the time, when a smoker walks by me, quietly
under my breath I utter, "Smoking can kill you. Didn't you
know that?" They look around wondering who said it. (Maybe
it was the cigarette talking?)

I wonder if they think about it later when they are
alone?

Remember it's only because I care.

*** Nicks ***

Nicks are dirty, smelly and dangerous pests. They
fester in trays about the house. They coat the surroundings
with their scum. The air stinks of their presence and the
stench follows one around. Nicks don't last long but they
multiply steadily, robbing their host of life and breath with
their excrement, odor and threat to life. Nicks should be
exterminated.

~ Author unknown

Part three summary

- ◆ See the humor in peer pressure.
- ◆ Be afraid of what will happen if you do not quit!
- ◆ Your subconscious does not know the difference between the truth and a lie...So lie!
- ◆ Format of tape recording.
- ◆ Content of what you will record.
- ◆ Remember the math to freedom.
- ◆ You can handle three weeks—It's the price to pay.
- ◆ Develop powerful mantras
- ◆ Turn in—Become empowered.
- ◆ Learn to have humour.
- ◆ Be excited about opening your "last pack".

Go for it!

I know you can do it!

If in doubt,
look in the mirror.

BMP Method

BARBARA MILLER'S PLAN™
BARBARA MILLER'S METHOD™

Part Four

Don't re-invent the wheel

Do **exactly** as I have.
Quitting will be easy

I WANT TO BE A NONSMOKER

CHECK THE ONES THAT YOU FEEL ARE IMPORTANT TO YOU.

♥ I want to live longer.
♥ I will feel healthier.
♥ My lungs will begin to heal and become cleaner.
♥ I will have more energy.
♥ My immune system will function more efficiently.
♥ My sleeping patterns will not be interrupted.
♥ Food will taste better.
♥ Without smoke breaks my time will be more productive.
♥ I will smell clean.
♥ The stains on my fingers will disappear.
♥ My teeth will become whiter.
♥ I will save hundreds and hundreds of dollars.
♥ I will be a role model to other smokers.
♥ I will be a role model for children.
♥ People will be proud of me.
♥ Without the addiction I will feel I'm in control of my life.
♥ I will have a great sense of accomplishment.
♥ My house, car and clothes will not stink.
♥ I will feel great inside about being a nonsmoker.
♥ The power to quit smoking will then be transferred to do other things I thought were too hard.
♥ If I can quit smoking I can do anything.
♥ The risk of cancer will be significantly reduced.

♥   I will feel **FREE.**
♥   I will be self-sufficient and relax on my own.
♥   I will be able to afford nice things for myself.
♥   I could save up my smoke money for a tropical vacation.
♥   My spouse, peers and family will admire me.
♥   My home and work environment will be healthier for pets, children, co-workers and the general public.

See if you can add to this list.

My Story

This story is about my struggle to quit for good. I started when I was fourteen. I can openly admit I had very low self-esteem and bought into the peer pressure. I wanted to be cool, so I picked one of the strongest brands. It was Export "A". The fact that smoking is dangerous also appealed to me. I was living on the edge. It tasted awful but hey, I was cool.

As I grew older it bothered me that I had surrendered to the "in crowd". It bothered me that I would risk my life for them, just to fit in. I built up resentment for the whole idea of changing in order to please others. When I was eighteen I thought I would fight back. I would take back my control, the control over just being myself. I looked at the whole thing like a game. I lost when I started to smoke. I would win when I quit! I wanted to win! I wanted to grow up and be healthy. I thought I would be the better for taking myself out of the "in crowd". I pictured them living with regret. I pictured me healthy and smiling.

The program you have done evolved from my three attempts at quitting forever. I knew why I wanted to quit. I knew what would motivate me as I have just explained. By doing the exercises, I was able to see smoking as bad and being a nonsmoker as good. This was my focus each time I quit.

Yes, I quit three times. Once when I was eighteen, for one year. At twenty-three I quit for two years. I started again at twenty-five and would smoke for another two years.

The cancer my dentist discovered was of my thyroid and not smoking related. As stupid as it is I started again even though I could get cancer. This is how I came up with my visualization story. I finally quit for good at twenty-seven. I have now been smoke-free for nine years. I have not taken one puff since then! I am healthy and free of cancer.

I examined what made me go back. Why did I light up again and again? This process took many years of trial and error. The missing ingredient was learning to relax on my own. Instead of running for smokes, I learned to go within. The self-hypnosis also helped clean out years of negative beliefs. This tape I made completely erased my old programming and gave me the opportunity to implant new and empowering ideas. I have done all the work that I am asking you to do. You can see it in my tape that follows, (pg 95) word for word...Yes some parts may seem humorous to you. It's OK, I hope you find it amusing. I also hope it inspires you to make one for yourself

My Personal Changes

DESTRUCTIVE EMPOWERING

I enjoy smoking.	I want good health.

This is quite the contradiction.
So I set out to deliberately change my thoughts.

HABITUAL THE NEW
THOUGHT SCRATCH THOUGHT

HABITUAL THOUGHT	THE SCRATCH	NEW THOUGHT
I enjoy smoking.	fear of dying overwhelming regret (review page 60) losers smoke (pain)	I want to be a healthy woman. I want to be a winner. (pleasure)

Quitting becomes easy when you find pleasure in what you will get.

It is harder to continue smoking when you're afraid of what will happen if you do not quit.

Barb's Personal Program

For all intent and purpose this tape will help me to quit smoking, but first I must get relaxed.

"Lay down in your favorite spot. Put your arms down beside you. Make sure your feet are not crossed. Do you feel comfortable? Focus on something at about an 80-degree angle above you. Gaze at it intently...Keep gazing and relax...your eyes are becoming watery...your eyes are becoming heavy...very watery...your eyes are becoming so heavy...keep gazing...so very heavy...close your eyes and relax... relax even deeper and deeper....take a deep breath......exhale slowly...let yourself go down deeper and deeper....go deep inside, down to your source of power... concentrate on relaxing and feeling comfortable...go deeper and deeper...you feel so comfortable and relaxed...you are almost there...

concentrate...feeling rested...you are at a relaxed state at 20...and feeling calm...19...very comfortable...18... going down deeper and deeper...

17... you are relaxed and happy where you are...16...going down...down...down...15...going deeper and deeper...14... you believe everything you hear on this recording... 13... my voice is the truth...the absolute truth...12...you will remember my words...11...so deep and so relaxed... 10...happy and free...9...relaxed and excited about not smoking anymore...8... take another deep breath...let it out slowly as you descend even deeper into a total state of relaxation...7...now feel how comfortable you are...6...

you feel great peace...you are safe...5...go deeper and hold onto your power...4...go even deeper to the depths of your mind...you feel light as air...you are floating as if on warm water...3...there it is...you can see your power... face it...embrace it... it is covering your whole body...2... you can feel your power taking over the situation...1...listen to your power...it is communicating to you now...your power says, I want to be a nonsmoker....(longer pause)

I believe that I have the power inside of me to break the chains of tar and nicotine...I am sick of it...I have inside...deep inside of me the power....I can feel it now...I can see it...

I remember the freedom I felt when I didn't smoke... it is a wonderful experience...I want to feel it again...I can do it...I will!

Smoking is so expensive...it cost me $120.00 a month to smoke if not more...I want to save some money... the stains on my fingers are so ugly...so unattractive...it really bothers me...I don't want it anymore...I meet many nonsmokers...

I feel cheap when I smoke around a good looking man...smoking is a threat to my life...I had cancer and I can get it again if I continue to smoke...I don't want to smoke anymore...

I smoke on the phone...when I drink tea or coffee, when I am nervous...after I do something like take a shower, when I am angry...I smoked mostly as a habit, something to do...just because I haven't in the recent past had the power to stop...doesn't mean anything today...I have the power now...

Things I can do to keep this power I have inside of me alive...I can start to exercise...I will start exercising...I'll do sit-ups, ride my bike, go for long walks...get healthy...I'll eat peanuts or sunflower seeds when I have the urge to smoke...I'll chew gum or eat breath fresheners because I want to put pleasant flavors in my mouth instead of the dirty dingy taste of tar and nicotine, that I know no one in their right mind would want to kiss.

I will learn how to relax in situations where I would normally smoke...I will not drink any alcohol until I have accomplished this task...I will leave home with no cigarettes... because I know I don't need them...I will use this power to brainwash myself because my brain has been stained with tar and nicotine...I will be excited about my new freedom... and not having cigarettes and smoke hanging around any more...

I am aware that this is a difficult, perhaps painful task that is not impossible to overcome. I will overcome this...I'm tired of it.

It cost too much...I don't want to smoke any more...I will remember these things when I wake up...I will think about this throughout the day...I will do this... smoking definitely reduces life expectancy...

If I ever had a baby the smoke would be harmful to it...once again I must express how incredibly expensive smoking is...it is a nast...nasty...habit...and a lot of good looking men have no place for it in their life...like me... I have no place for it in my life...I will save money...tons of it...I can party, go buy clothes and feel rich because I don't smoke because people who quit are rich with power....the power to quit is an incredible source of power and everyday that I don't smoke is a day that I walk around with that power tucked away.

Once again the stains on my fingers are so ugly, and it is so hard to take off...when I quit smoking, which I will do...I won't have that problem anymore...it will be a thing of the past...my future is full of the sense of freedom of what I have accomplished...I have had this feeling before... only an ex smoker can know this feeling as they have been tied to the chains of being addicted.

I feel terrible when I meet a good looking man and I happen to have a cigarette hanging out of my mouth...I'm sure I look cheap...the smell is on my clothes...and in my mouth...probably in my hair...I need to put on so much perfume in order to cover up the smell of smoke...it gets on everything...I want to have a long and healthy well lived life...there cannot be any room in there for smoke... smoking is mostly a habit anyway...a habit I don't need... it's not really an addiction...it was just something to do... unless you're smoking because you're nervous or mad and that just means you're being weak...if I don't smoke in those situations I am exercising my power... it is a difficult process to go through but it is not impossible to overcome it...

I feel strong that I will overcome it this time once and for all...give it up...break the chains...feel free... happy...and excited like a monkey is lifted off my back with a $ sign attached to it...it is so stupid to spend $4.00 on a pack of smokes...it is just like taking $4.00 and rolling it up into a smoke and having burnt ash-money left over…it is an amazing habit but not impossible to stop.

Drinking when trying to quit is fruitless…I can not quit smoking if I continue to drink…it's easy to say no to a drink especially when it is for something as important as freeing myself from the chains of smoking…I'd much rather not drink for a couple of weeks than to smoke for the rest of my life…it stinks…it's ugly…it is a bad, bad, habit…I don't want it anymore…

When I open my eyes I will remember all that I am saying and believe… I will feel relaxed…exited and happy about what I am doing…I know what I am doing is possible…I will have this power with me at all times…it will not hurt to go out of the house without cigarettes…it won't hurt not smoking at work…I know I can eventually go to parties without smokes…I will meet good looking guys who appreciate a nonsmoking woman…

You can do it Barb…you have the power now!… exercise…this power…use it throughout the day…you will remember these words and feel powerful…can you feel the sense of accomplishment burning inside of you?"

Intermission: song by Bette Midler: "Wind beneath my Wings," (Approximately 45-50 seconds.)

Part two....
"That's what it will be like not to smoke…like flying free, with the wind beneath my wings… I will fly high with the sense of accomplishment…it is the power that is the wind

beneath my wings...

It is so powerful...it is stronger than your own mind... it will make you fly...you will have no chains to tie you down... no stinky smoke... no habit...no smell, no stains...just the sense of freedom...it is so enormous you'll think you can fly...

Don't forget about the exercising, the sit-ups and riding your bike...get healthy!...munch on peanuts and sun flower seeds...chew gum and eat candy like certs for putting flavor in your mouth, instead of the dingy taste of tar and nicotine...learn how to relax when you feel like a smoke... because you do not want to smoke any more...do you?...if you want a cigarette learn how to relax without it!...leave home without them because you don't need them anymore... don't buy any more packages...even that is a habit ...you will have to learn new ways when you are at the store buying milk...get a treat for yourself instead...concentrate on the sense of freedom that you will have as a nonsmoker...it feels so good to be free...you will be flying high...high on life with a sense of happiness and a sense of accomplishment... the wind beneath your wings is the power that will make you want to quit smoking...it will lift you to your new life... YOU DON'T WANT TO SMOKE... YOU DON'T WANT CIGARETTES... you don't want to smoke any more you're tired of it... you have quit before twice and can do it again... with the help of the power that is inside of you...that is controlling your mind...it is so much stronger than a $4.00 pack of smokes...

You are still relaxed and comfortable, concentrating on these words, and knowing that in your heart you do not want to smoke anymore...you have no use for cigarettes.

The smell...the urge will pass when you feel it... it will come and it will go...because you have the power... you have memorized my words...it will be a challenge but I know you can do it...it is possible to quit and go through the process... when you want a smoke know that you don't really want a cigarette, but that it is an urge that surges but will pass...like gas...gone...out...over with...pick up a book or work on a puzzle, go for a walk, or exercise...just do something...even lie back and practice relaxing... strive to be **#**1 as a nonsmoker...you can imagine life ahead with more money...better health, happier, with a sense of freedom because you have gone through the rebirth of quitting smoking...difficult times don't last... it is only a brief discomfort...think of passing gas or passing the time... or a passing moment in a long life...take your mind off of the discomfort like you do when you have a headache...do something...know it will pass...it is not something you will feel 24hrs a day...it does pass...you know because you have experienced this process before and you will do it again...

This power doesn't come by very often...it could be a long time before it comes this way again...use it now while you have it...feel free...don't smoke... get the monkey that is laughing off your back... you will be relaxed and refreshed and not want to smoke when you open your eyes... you will be happy and excited and go and do something positive without cigarettes because you don't want them or need themanymore...you know this to be true...you know this to be a fact...you know my words only speak the truth... the whole truth and nothing but the truth...your power is there and will never leave you...it will get you through the difficult times...and so will the peanuts and the sunflower seeds, and gum and good looking men who don't smoke... most of the best looking men out there don't smoke...it is because they are into health and they want a healthy woman too...you can be that woman...Barb...don'tgive up...fight...kick...scream...struggle...but don't smoke anymore!...GIVE IT UP! ...

The urge for wanting a cigarette is leaving now... you know if you had one it would taste terrible...I would much rather have some candy or gum...

Life is too short to be wasting it standing in line for smokes...it is a disgusting filthy habit...you know that to be true... so do all the other nonsmokers...join them...be a part of the team...BUTT/OUT! time to start a new way of living... a new life!"

Intermission: "God is Watching Us," by Bette Midler. (40 seconds)

Part three

And he'll see you if you light up...he'll be watching... he doesn't want you to light up...you don't want to light up either...so don't! ... give it up!

Until next time butt out...that's it. I QUIT..."

Encouraging music on the end of my tape is: Entire song:

- Billy Ocean—*When The Going Gets Tough*, (the tough get going.)
- Dennis Deyoung— *Don't Wait for Heroes*
- Patty Labelle — *I Got a New Attitude*
- Loverboy— *Turn Me Loose*

"You have the power to turn that nasty habit loose...LET IT GO!...turn it loose...you have a new attitude...a nonsmoker attitude...you have this power... you don't need to wait for heroes...the time is now!... no time like the present... you don't want to smoke anymore Barb...give it up...QUIT!...STOP... YOU DON'T WANT TO SMOKE...YOU DON'T WANT A CIGARETTE... YOU DON'T WANT TO SMOKE ANYMORE! ... say goodbye to an old habit... turn it loose ...you have a new attitude...you are not going to wait for heroes...nobody is going to help you but yourself...

Have a good rest...wake up and go do something... stay active...go and live your life... until we meet again... by for now

I QUIT".

That's my contents of my recording. I know it is repetitive. This is required for the brain to absorb. Remember that the second hardest part of quitting smoking is remembering that you have made this decision. You must drill this message into the brain! The pause... like that one...is varied in length. Some are five seconds some are ten. It doesn't matter as long as you space it out so as to use your whole tape. If you record your tape and you find that when you are done there is half a tape left, then you need to re-do it and make the pauses longer.

I quit smoking many years ago . The inspirational music I used is very old. Find some break up songs that you like and use them for inspiration.

You must not raise your voice. USE A TONE OF PURE DETERMINATION.

Put more emphasis on key points that are extra important.

A Smoker's Testimony

30 years and two packs a day

I have tried many different ways to quit smoking and nothing has ever worked for me. The patches, the gum and the pills, I have tried them all. All I got from those things were sleepless nights or an upset stomach or just the worst taste in my mouth. Also I experienced high stress and anger. I never seemed able to get smoking out of my mind. I really talked a good talk but I never was able to get over the top. One night in February of 1999 some friends of mine and I were outside having a smoke during an industry function. When we came back into the building I made a remark that I really wished I could quit. As I was saying this we passed a lady who was standing there and she commented that I should try her method. That stopped me with the utmost curiosity. She then explained her method. I took her card and left. Curiosity made me go back to talk to her about what she had just said and she started to explain to me and several of my friends what the BMP. Method was all about. She really got my attention. I kept thinking about what she had said to me and her program was not like any of the rest. She supports and coaches you throughout the program. When she told me that I could keep on smoking while doing the program, I thought that would be great. Well, she was right. I did continue to smoke as I stayed with the program and I am happy to say that I have not had a cigarette in 22 days. Not very long you say? Well, for a guy who has smoked 30 to 40 cigarettes every day for the last 30 years, I'll tell you that 22 days is a very long time. I know now that in another 22 days it will be 44 days since I quit.

I found Barbara Miller's method made quitting smoking easier than I thought possible. Barb's method worked for me and those people who want to quit, should take a look at Barb's plan.

Up until the night I met Barb in early February, 1999 I thought I would go through the rest of my life being a smoker. I feel I owe her so very much for being herself and for what both she and the BMP Method have given me. I am 49 years old and I feel that I have been given a second chance on life. I intend to enjoy my new life as a non-smoker to the fullest.

I am a satisfied client and highly recommend her method. "Barb's plan" worked and will continue to work for me.

Thank you Barb,
I owe you so much.

Brian Mons

As of April, 2000
Brian is still not smoking.

Be On Guard

IF ALL ELSE FAILS
TWIDDLE YOUR THUMBS.

I'm Just Kidding!

However, you may wonder what to do with your hands when you have quit. I did in fact twiddle my thumbs. I also ate too much food. In hindsight I wish I had picked healthier snacks. Be on guard: Putting your hand to your mouth is also a major habit. After you quit you will still have this urge. By being on guard and being prepared you can make a decision now to eat healthy snacks foods. I did gain weight mostly because of poor choices. I thought heck, if I can quit smoking I can do anything, including lose weight.

I'm fit for life and I exercise regularly.

When you are out in public places such as clubs, pubs, parties or dances, consider twisting a small piece of paper lightly with both hands. (I still do.) The paper is so small no one can hardly tell I'm fiddling. It just gives my fingers something to play with.

Go ahead!
Find something to fiddle with.

Final Thoughts

The BMP Method is contained in the contents of this book and it is in the application of all the exercises.

If you did not do all of the work contained in this book your chances of making quitting easier will be greatly impaired.

When you quit please say the BMP Method worked for you.

If you have not been successful and you did not do all that you were asked to do please do not condemn the method.

Admit you did not follow through.

Thank You

Let's make this a smoke free world.

Barbara Miller travels the globe doing her fast paced high energy workshop.

Check www.quitsmokingbmp.com to find out when she will be in your area.

Contact   **BMP Productions**
                 875 Admirals Rd.
                 Victoria B.C.
                 V9A 2A3

                 Toll free at 1-866-383-9087

Barbara would love to hear from you. Please send your letters and questions to the above address or email bmpmethod@shaw.ca

Do not be afraid of quitting
Be afraid of what will happen if you do not!

You are out camping. You go for a hike. All of a sudden you stumble across a grizzly bear! You start running for your life. You run and run. There you are, nowhere to go but over a cliff and into the lake below. You're terrified! You're afraid of heights! The bear is charging at you! Someone yells, "JUMP!" You know you must. You take a deep breath, close your eyes and jump! Splash! You did it! You jumped. You made it! You are so happy you got away from that beast. The water is nice so you stay and splash around as you enjoy the moment of triumph.

**Quitting smoking
is like a jump.**

**Go ahead,
JUMP!**

I DID IT!

About the Author

Born and raised in Prince George. Barbara was raised with her father as the primary care giver with her two older brothers. Faced with adversity from a very young age she grew up with an ability to be strong and rise above extraordinary difficult situations. One of the most difficult challenges she faced is found at www.quitsmokingbmp.com and is noted there as evidence that Barbara knows a thing a two about overcoming obstacles.

Barbara shaped herself into exactly the kind of person she wanted to be with the goal of rising above circumstances in order to show others that anything really is possible. This was done by studying at home with self improvement books for the course of twenty years. The accumulative information lived out year after year has made her the person she is today.

Barbara smoked for thirteen years in total and that included starting again after having cancer surgery. She started smoking very young and quit the first time at eighteen for one year, next time she quit for two years. She started again and examined her method. She added two things to the program and now in 2007 it has been seventeen years without even one puff!

Happy and well adjusted Barbara enjoys her life in Victoria B.C. Canada. Working hard and also enjoying the time to enjoy the journey.

ISBN 1552123448

9 781552 123447